Selected Duets

for SAXOPHONE

Published in Two Volumes:

VOLUME I (Easy-Medium)

• VOLUME II (Advanced)

Compiled and Edited

by H. VOXMAN

Preface

Duet playing affords the student the most intimate form of ensemble experience. The problems of technic, tone quality, intonation, and ensemble balance are brought into the sharpest relief. Careful attention must be given to style as indicated by the printed page and as demanded by the intangibles of good taste.

Mastery of the art of duet playing leads easily and naturally to competent performance in the larger ensembles. The numerous works included in this volume have been selected for the purpose of introducing the saxophonist to the finest in two-part ensemble literature and acquainting him with a diversity of musical forms and expressions.

H. Voxman

Minuetto

BEETHOVEN

mf
dim.
p
cresc.
f
1
2
Fine
TRIO
pp
Da Capo
Minuetto

Petite Sonate No. 1, Op. 13

BOISMORTIER

ALLEMANDE

* = Short trill beginning on upper auxiliary.

COURANTE

GIGUE

LUFT

p
a tempo
p
sf
sf
legato
cresc.
sf
sf
sf
sf
sf
dim.
p dolce
p
cresc.
fp

f
f
f
f
p
p
fp
p
p
pp
pp
cresc.
p
p
dim.
f
f

Sonata 6

TELEMANN

Canonic Sonata No. 4

TELEMANN

The second player begins each section when the first player has reached the sign (𝄋).

The second player finishes each section at the first fermata (𝄐), which should not be observed by the first player.

Piacevole non Largo
p
segue

Presto
mf

QUANTZ

p
f
[f]
tr
[tr]

[tr]
[tr]
tr
tr
tr
tr
tr
tr

CROFT

KLOSÉ
Allegro non troppo
8
f
f
p
p

f
f
p
p
dolce

légèrement

Allegretto
GEMINIANI
9
p
p
f
f
p
p
cresc.
cresc.
tr
f
f
f
f
sfz
sfz
mf
mf
cresc.
cresc.
f
sfz
sfz

mf
mf
f
f
p
p
cresc.
cresc.
p
p
f
f
p
p
cresc.
cresc.
tr
tr
f
f
tr

From Duetto No. IV

W. F. BACH

* When ♪. ♬ is played against a triplet, play it ♩ 3 ♪

p
f
p
f
p
f
p
dim.
f
dim.
p
p
cresc.
cresc.
mf
mf
cresc.
cresc.
f
f

Rondo - Minuetto

FERLING

Fine
segue

C. STAMITZ

fp
fp
p
p
[p]
[p]
p
f
f
f
p
fp
fp
fp
p
p

Duetto V

f
p
sf
tr

Ger Falk

Dialog

p
cresc.
f
p
cresc.
f
p
p
ff

ff
ff
ff
rit.

SELLNER
Adagio con espressione
16
p
sf
f
cre - - scen - - - do
p

BACH - COMBELLE

Duo Récréatif

COMBELLE

mf
f
f
pp
cresendo
p
p
pp
pizzicati
pp

Invention

sf
f
p
f
f

Divertissement

RICHARD HERVIG

Allegro (♩ = 152)
mf
mf
p
p
fp
fp
fp
fp
fp
fp
f
fp
f
mf
fp
f
f
f
f
f
p
f
f
p
f
fp
fp
p
f
p
f
p
f
p
f
p
cresc.
f
p
cresc.
p cresc.
p cresc.
f
p
f
p

espr.
mf espr.
Solo
cresc.

dim.
ritard.
a tempo
p
p
p
p
fp
mf
p
p
p
p
cresc.
cresc.
fp
fp
fp
fp
f
f
p cresc.
p cresc.
f
f

Duo

C. P. E. BACH

Duet No. 3

Based on Sonata, K 454

MOZART

Largo [in eight]

22

f *p dol.* *f* *f* *p* *f* Solo

dol. Solo *p cresc.* *p*

p *sfp* *sfp* *p*

p Solo *mf* Solo *mf* *p* *p* Attacca

Allegro
p
dolce
p
f
f
f
f
rfz
rfz
rfz
Solo
mf
dol.
Solo
p

Solo
dol.

dol.
f
p
f
p dol.
p
p dol.
p
f
p
p dol.
dol.
cresc.
cresc.
p
cresc.
p
p
cresc.
cresc.
cresc.
cresc.

dol.
dol.
p
p
cresc.
cresc.
f
f
f
f
rfz
f
rfz
rfz
rfz
rfz
rfz
rfz
f

mf Solo
Solo

p dol.
p Solo
f
p
f
p dol.
f
p
f
p
p
p
dol.
dol.
mf
mf
f
f
attacca

RONDO

Allegretto con moto
mf
p dol.
Solo
mf
p dol.
f
f
dol.

f
f
f
f
p dol.
p dol.
cresc.
cresc.
f
rfz
rfz
rfz

f
p dol.
cresc.
f
p dol.
cresc.
f
f
p dol.
p dol.
f
f
mf
p dol.

rfz
rfz
rfz
rfz
tr
tr
tr
tr
p dol.
p dol.
mf
p
Solo
mf

p
f
f
mf
p dol.
cresc.
cresc.
f
f
p dol.
p dol.

cresc.
cresc.
cresc.
cresc.
mf
mf
p dol.
mf
mf

cresc.
cresc.
mf
rfz
rfz
rfz
rfz
rfz
f
dol.
dol.
dim.
p
mf
dim.
p

dol.
dol.
p
p
dol.
dol.
p
p
f
mf
tr

MOZART
Andante con variazioni
23
p
dol.
VARIATION I
3

VARIATION II
dol.
dol.
VARIATION III
dol.
f
f
dol.
dol.
f
f
dol.
mf
dol.

Duo

Based on Sonata, K 379

MOZART

f
dol.
dol.
p
p
cresc.
cresc.
mf
mf
p
p
f
f
p
p
cresc.
rfz
f
f
rfz
p
p

Allegro
cresc.
rall
en
tando
Allegro
cresc.
rall
en
tando
Allegro
dol.

rfz
rfz
rfz
rfz
p dol.
p dol.
f
cresc.
tr
f
segue

p
p
cresc.
cresc.
f
p
cresc.
p
f
f
rfz
tr
p
p
rall
cresc.
en
tan
do
f
f
f
f

Allegro
p dol.
p dol.
cresc.
f
rfz
rfz
rfz
rfz
f
rfz

rfz
f
tr
p dol.
p dol.
f
f
rfz
rfz
rfz
tr
ff
ff